CENTURY OF CLOUDS

Davie.

Best wishes

Wendy

22 January 1986

GEOFF PAGE
and
WENDY COUTTS

CENTURY OF CLOUDS

Selected Poems from the French of
GUILLAUME APOLLINAIRE

1985
THE LEROS PRESS
Canberra, Australia

Typeset by The Typesetting Centre, Allara Street, Canberra.
Printed and bound by Paragon Printers Pty Ltd, Fyshwick.

Published with the assistance of
the Commonwealth Schools Commission.

ISBN 0 949264 16 4

PREFACE

By any account Guillaume Apollinaire (1880-1918) was a spectacular individual: friend and proponent of the Cubists; coiner of the term surrealism; writer of some of the most delicate of French lyrics; sometime pornographic novelist; patriot and war hero — and that is just one catalogue. Even were his poems to be set aside, Apollinaire would still have to be regarded as one of the great 'characters' of modern French culture.

The present translations from his work began in both fascination and frustration: fascination with such a mercurial and charming personality; frustration with the few English translations of his work available. Judging simply from these it was difficult to see what all the excitement was about. Very few of them gave even a hint of Apollinaire's distinctive verbal music; most seemed to portray him (unintentionally, no doubt) as a fevered romantic whose somewhat impetuous technique invariably meant that his poems fell well short of the potential of their best lines.

Believing that any poet should be judged by his best work rather than his occasional trifles or grand failures, we have compiled a selection which should do a little more justice to the sense of bravura and style one gets from his biographies. A few major poems such as 'Zone' and 'La Chanson du Mal-Aimé' have already been effectively translated elsewhere and were thus omitted. The present selection shows Apollinaire in several of his more effective veins — in particular, the early poems from his year in the Rhineland (1901–2) and the best of his completely individual poems from the Western Front. The typographic poems in *Calligrammes* have been largely ignored for both practical and aesthetic reasons. While these were the charming spontaneous gestures a prophet of the New might be expected to make, they are rarely as affecting as his more subtle experiments in the conventional framework of the line-by-line poem.

In these translations we have tried to avoid both excessive literalness (which gives no sense of any style, let alone Apollinaire's) and excessive freedom (whereby a new poem is created with only a vague bow in the direction of the original). Our aim throughout has been a good poem in English, while remaining as close to the style of the French as possible. When the inevitable conflicts arose we invariably opted for what sounded best in English. There are, therefore, occasional changes in the tense and person of verbs, a few reversals of line order, and a word or two omitted altogether. It hardly seems likely that a poet of Apollinaire's flair and adventurousness would be satisfied with anything more cautious.

These English versions were developed by Geoff Page from (with one exception) the literal translations of Wendy Coutts and were then checked over by a native French speaker. Naturally, in the case of a poet as playful with language as Apollinaire is, the translator frequently has to settle for one (or, at best, two) meanings of a word or phrase which in the French might have several more. These are undeniable losses but hardly sufficient reason for leaving Apollinaire as the exclusive property of the fluent French speaker. As this selection should demonstrate, he is too large a poet for that.

Geoff Page and Wendy Coutts

Chronology

1880	August 26. Born Guglielmo Dulcigni to Mme Angelica de Kostrowitsky and (probably) Francesco Fluigi d'Aspermont, an Italian army officer; in Rome.
1887-1897	Educated (with younger brother, Albert) in various Catholic schools in Monte Carlo, Nice and Cannes while mother worked as an *entraîneuse* in gambling casinos.
1899	Flight with brother Albert from hotel in Stavelot (Eastern Belgium) to Paris, without paying bill; charge of fraud later dropped.
1900-1901	Odd jobs in Paris; first literary contacts.
1901-1902	Tutor to daughter of Vicomtesse de Milhau at Honnef-on-Rhine, near Bonn; fell in love with Annie Playden, an English governess in the same house.
1902-1907	Worked as a clerk in various small banks in Paris; lived with mother and brother.
1903	November. Trip to London to see Annie Playden.
1903-1904	Founded and edited magazine *Festin d'Esope*; published major poems 'La Chanson du Mal-Aimé' and 'L'Emigrant de Landor Road'.
1904-1905	Met Picasso, Vlaminck and André Derain (and was later associated with most of the major artists in Paris in the pre-war period).
1907	*Les Onze Milles Verges* (pornographic novel; published anonymously).

1907	Began liaison with Marie Laurencin, the painter.
1909	*L'Enchanteur Pourrissant*; illustrated by André Derain; (poetry and prose based on the Arthurian legends).
1910	*L'Héresiarque et Cie* (stories).
1911	*Le Bestiaire*; illustrated by Raoul Dufy; (poetry).
1911	Began literary and artistic gossip column for *Mercure de France*, 'La Vie Anecdotique'.
1911	Wrongfully arrested and held for four days in jail on suspicion of harbouring the thief who stole the Mona Lisa from the Louvre.
1912	Split up with Marie Laurencin.
1913	*Les Peintres Cubistes*; (writings on art).
1913	*Alcools* (poetry); first major collection; 350 copies sold in first year; over a hundred editions since.
1914	August 10. Applied for enlistment in French army; accepted in December 1914; rose to lieutenant within a few months.
1914	October-December. Short affair with 'Lou' (Louise de Coligny-Châtillon) followed by correspondence.
1915	January 1. Met Madeleine Pagès, sometime fiancée and recipient of much of his wartime correspondence.
1915	May. Sent to Western Front; initially in artillery, then in infantry as a second lieutenant.

1915	December. Two weeks leave spent at Oran (Algeria) with Madeleine Pagès, then his fiancée.
1916	March 9. Granted French citizenship.
1916	March 17. Wounded in the head by fragments from a shell-burst while reading *Mercure de France*; several head operations including trepanning.
1916-1918	Appointed a wartime censor, especially concerned with little magazines; continued writing.
1916	*Le Poète Assassiné* (prose; semi-autobiographical).
1917	Performance of his play, *Les Mamelles de Tirésias*, a 'surrealist drama'.
1918	January. Bout of pneumonia.
1918	April. *Calligrammes* (poetry); a second major collection.
1918	May 2. Married Jacqueline Kolb ('La Jolie Russe').
1918	July. Promoted to first lieutenant (while still in Paris).
1918	November 9. Died of 'Spanish grippe', having been weakened by pneumonia and his head operations.

Contents

Acknowledgments

All poems except two are taken from the Gallimard editions of *Alcools* and *Calligrammes*. 'Inscription pour le tombeau du peintre Henri Rousseau' is from *Le Guetteur Mélancolique* (Gallimard). 'Souvenir du Douanier' is quoted in Dora Vallier's *Henri Rousseau*, Thames and Hudson, London 1967.

The translators would like to thank Erika Gaudlitz for her assistance with 'Souvenir du Douanier' and Makar Press which published *Collecting the Weather* where four of these poems first appeared. Acknowledgment is also made to the *Bulletin*, *Meanjin*, *New Poetry* and *Quadrant* in which some of these translations have previously appeared.

Particular thanks are due to Françoise Lentsch and James Grieve who kindly scrutinised the finished manuscript; however they must bear no responsibility for the final form of the translations.

Grateful acknowledgment is made to the Commonwealth Schools Commission for its financial assistance through a grant under its Projects of National Significance Program.

RHÉNANE D'AUTOMNE

à Toussaint-Luca

Les enfants des morts vont jouer
Dans le cimetière
Martin Gertrude Hans et Henri
Nul coq n'a chanté aujourd'hui
Kikiriki

Les vieilles femmes
Tout en pleurant cheminent
Et les bons ânes
Braillent hi han et se mettent à brouter les fleurs
Des couronnes mortuaires

C'est le jour des morts et de toutes leurs âmes
Les enfants et les vieilles femmes
Allument des bougies et des cierges
Sur chaque tombe catholique
Les voiles des vieilles
Les nuages du ciel
Sont commes des barbes de biques

L'air tremble de flammes et de prières

RHENISH AUTUMN

for Toussaint-Luca

The children of the dead go out to play
In the cemetery
Martin Gertrude Hans and Henri
No rooster crowed today
Kikiriki

Old women
In tears make their way also
And the good donkeys go
Hi-haw beginning to browse
On remembrance flowers

It's the day of the dead with all their souls
Old women and children
Light candles and tapers
On each Catholic grave
The veils of old women
The clouds in the sky
Are just like a nanny goat's beard

The air is trembling with flames and prayers

Le cimetière est un beau jardin
Plein de saules gris et de romarins
Il vous vient souvent des amis qu'on enterre
Ah! que vous êtes bien dans le beau cimetière
Vous mendiants morts saouls de bière
Vous les aveugles comme le destin
Et vous petits enfants morts en prière

Ah! que vous êtes bien dans le beau cimetière
Vous bourgmestres vous bateliers
Et vous conseillers de régence
Vous aussi tziganes sans papiers
La vie vous pourrit dans la panse
La croix vous pousse entre les pieds

Le vent du Rhin ulule avec tous les hiboux
Il éteint les cierges que toujours les enfants rallument
Et les feuilles mortes
Viennent couvrir les morts

Des enfants morts parlent parfois avec leur mère
Et des mortes parfois voudraient bien revenir

Oh! je ne veux pas que tu sortes
L'automne est plein de mains coupées
Non non ce sont des feuilles mortes
Ce sont les mains des chères mortes
Ce sont tes mains coupées

The cemetery is a wonderful garden
Full of grey willows and rosemary
You're visited often by friends who are buried
In the beautiful graveyard you're doing fine
You beggars down there dead drunk with your beer
You blind men blind as fate
You little children dying in prayer

You're doing fine yes in the beautiful graveyard
You burgers you boatmen
You brokers of state
You gypsies without any papers
Life decays you in the gut
The cross thrusts up between your feet

The wind off the Rhine is hooting with owls
It blows out the tapers the children relight
And the dead leaves
Come to cover the dead

Dead children speak sometimes with their mothers
And dead women sometimes would like to come back
Please don't go out
The autumn is full of severed hands
No these are just dead leaves
They are the hands of long-loved women
They are your severed hands.

Nous avons tant pleuré aujourd'hui
Avec ces morts leurs enfants et les vieilles femmes
Sous le ciel sans soleil
Au cimetière plein de flammes

Puis dans le vent nous nous en retournâmes
A nos pieds roulaient des châtaignes
Dont les bogues étaient
Comme le coeur blessé de la madone
Dont on doute si elle eut la peau
Couleur des châtaignes d'automne

We have wept so much today
With the dead for their children and the aged women
Under the sky without a sun
In the graveyard full of flames

Then in the wind we returned
And rolling at our feet were chestnuts
Whose husks were like
The wounded heart of the madonna
One doubts if even she had skin
The colour of chestnuts in autumn

LES SAPINS

Les sapins en bonnets pointus
De longues robes revêtus
Commes des astrologues
Saluent leurs frères abattus
Les bateaux qui sur le Rhin voguent

Dans les sept arts endoctrinés
Par les vieux sapins leurs aînés
        Qui sont de grands poètes
Ils se savent prédestinés
A briller plus que des planètes

A briller doucement changés
En étoiles et enneigés
        Aux Noëls bienheureuses
Fêtes des sapins ensongés
Aux longues branches langoureuses

Les sapins beaux musiciens
Chantent de noëls anciens
        Au vent des soirs d'automne
Ou bien graves magiciens
Incantent le ciel quand il tonne

Des rangées de blancs chérubins
Remplacent l'hiver les sapins
        Et balancent leurs ailes
L'été ce sont de grands rabbins
Ou bien de vieilles demoiselles

FIR TREES

Fir trees in their pointed bonnets
And long gowns
Of astrologers
Salute their fallen brothers
Boats which sail on the Rhine

Instructed in the seven arts
By old fir trees their elders
Who are great poets
They know themselves ordained
To far outshine the planets

To shine transformed
By snow as stars
At joyful Christmasses
Seasons full of the thoughtful firs
With languorous long branches

Fir trees beautiful musicians
Sing the carols of long ago
In the wind of autumn evenings
Or as serious magicians
Chant to thunder in the sky

Cherubim in long white rows
Stand in for them all through the winter
Balancing their wings
In summer they are lofty rabbis
Or maybe aged spinsters

Sapins médecins divagants
Ils vont offrant leurs bons onguents
        Quand la montagne accouche
De temps en temps sous l'ouragan
Un vieux sapin geint et se couche

The fir trees wandering physicians
Offer their salves
When the mountain's in labour
From time to time beneath the storm
An old fir tree will groan and fall

AUTOMNE MALADE

Automne malade et adoré
Tu mourras quand l'ouragan soufflera dans les roseraies
Quand il aura neigé
Dans les vergers

Pauvre automne
Meurs en blancheur et en richesse
De neige et de fruits mûrs
Au fond du ciel
Des éperviers planent
Sur les nixes nicettes aux cheveux verts et naines
Qui n'ont jamais aimé

Aux lisières lointaines
Les cerfs ont bramé

Et que j'aime ô saison que j'aime tes rumeurs
Les fruits tombant sans qu'on les cueille
Le vent et la forêt qui pleurent
Toutes leurs larmes en automne feuille à feuille
        Les feuilles
        Qu'on foule
        Un train
        Qui roule
        La vie
        S'écoule

SICK AUTUMN

Autumn dying yet beloved
You will be gone when the storm blows through the roses
And the snow
Is in the orchards

Die poor autumn
In the whiteness and wealth
Of snow and the ripened fruit
Almost in heaven
The sparrow hawks glide
Over nymphs with green hair
Who have never loved

At the forest's far edges
The stags have belled
O season I love the sounds that I love
Of windfalling fruit that will never be gathered
The wind and the forest weeping
All their tears in autumn leaf by leaf

The leaves
Which are trampled
A wheel
That turns
The life
Which is running out

LES COLCHIQUES

Le pré est vénéneux mais joli en automne
Les vaches y paissant
Lentement s'empoisonnent
Le colchique couleur de cerne et de lilas
Y fleurit tes yeux sont comme cette fleur-là
Violâtres comme leur cerne et comme cet automne
Et ma vie pour tes yeux lentement s'empoisonne

Les enfants de l'école viennent avec fracas
Vêtus de hoquetons et jouant de l'harmonica
Ils cueillent les colchiques qui sont commes des mères
Filles de leurs filles et sont couleur de tes paupières
Qui battent comme les fleurs battent au vent dément

Le gardien du troupeau chante tout doucement
Tandis que lentes et meuglant les vaches abandonnent
Pour toujours ce grand pré mal fleuri par l'automne

LES COLCHIQUES*

The meadow is deadly but pretty in autumn
The cows grazing there
Are slowly being poisoned
Colchique the colour of eye shadow or of lilac
Your eyes are like that flower in bloom
Mauvish as its ring of colour and like this autumn
And my life which for your eyes is slowly being poisoned

Children come from school with their commotion
Dressed in smocks and playing harmonicas
They gather the colchiques which are like their mothers
Daughters of their daughters and the colour of your eyelids
That quiver like flowers in a maddened wind

The cowherd sings softly
As the lowing cows abandon slowly and forever
This huge field of flowers
Made deadly by autumn

* Wild flower like a crocus, poisonous when in bloom.

AUTOMNE

Dans le brouillard s'en vont un paysan cagneux
Et son boeuf lentement dans le brouillard d'automne
Qui cache les hameaux pauvres et vergogneux

Et s'en allant là-bas le paysan chantonne
Une chanson d'amour et d'infidélité
Qui parle d'une bague et d'une coeur que l'on brise

Oh! l'automne l'automne a fait mourir l'été
Dans le brouillard s'en vont deux silhouettes grises

AUTUMN

Into the fog goes the knock-kneed peasant
With his ox slowly in the fog of autumn
That covers the sad and threadbare hamlets

And as he goes the peasant hums
A song of love and faithlessness
That speaks of a ring and a broken heart

Autumn oh! autumn that made the summer die
Into the fog go two grey shadows

LES FEMMES

Dans la maison du vigneron les femmes cousent
Lenchen remplis le poêle et mets l'eau du café
Dessus — Le chat s'étire après s'être chauffé
— Gertrude et son voisin Martin enfin s'épousent

Le rossignol aveugle essaya de chanter
Mais l'effraie ululant il trembla dans sa cage
Ce cyprès là-bas a l'air du pape en voyage
Sous la neige — Le facteur vient de s'arrêter

Pour causer avec le nouveau maître d'école
— Cet hiver est très froid le vin sera très bon
— Le sacristain sourd et boiteux est moribond
— La fille du vieux bourgmestre brode une étole

Pour la fête du curé La forêt là-bas
Grâce au vent chantait à voix grave de grand orgue
Le songe Herr Traum survint avec sa soeur Frau Sorge
Kaethi tu n'as pas bien raccommodé ces bas

— Apporte le café le beurre et les tartines
La marmelade le saindoux un pot de lait
— Encore un peu de café Lenchen s'il te plaît
— On dirait que le vent dit des phrases latines

THE WOMEN

In the winegrower's house the women are sewing
Lenchen stoke up the stove put on the coffee
— The cat stretches out all warm from the fire
— Gertrude and her neighbour Martin at last
are getting married

The blinded nightingale tried out a note
But when the night-owl screamed he trembled in his cage
That cypress there has the air of a pope
Travelling under the snow — The postman has just stopped by

To chat with the new schoolmaster
— This winter is cold and the wine will be good
— The sexton is deaf and lame and dying
— The old mayor's daughter embroiders a stole

For the priest on his name-day The forest out there
By grace of the wind is singing a deep organ note
Herr Dream calls in with his sister Frau Sorrow
Kaethi these socks are not darned very well

— Bring out the coffee and bread-and-butter
Marmalade lard and a pitcher of milk
— A little more coffee Lenchen please
The wind it seems is speaking Latin

— Encore un peu de café Lenchen s'il te plaît
— Lotte es-tu triste O petit coeur — Je crois qu'elle aime
— Dieu garde — Pour ma part je n'aime que moi-même
— Chut A présent grand-mère dit son chapelet

— Il me faut du sucre candi Leni je tousse
— Pierre mène son furet chasser les lapins
Le vent faisait danser en rond tous les sapins
Lotte l'amour rend triste — Ilse la vie est douce

La nuit tombait Les vignobles aux ceps tordus
Devenaient dans l'obscurité des ossuaires
En neige et repliés gisaient là des suaires
Et des chiens aboyaient aux passants morfondus

Il est mort écoutez La cloche de l'église
Sonnait tout doucement la mort du sacristain
Lise il faut attiser le poêle qui s'éteint
Les femmes se signaient dans la nuit indécise

A little more coffee Lenchen please
— Are you sad Lotte my little heart — Could it be love
— God help you — I for one love only myself
— Ssh grandmother's saying her rosary

— Pass me some candy Leni I'm coughing
— There goes Pierre with his ferret hunting
The wind made the fir-trees dance in a circle
Lotte love is sad — Ilse life is sweet

Night was coming down The vineyard's twisted stems
Became in the darkness heaps of bones
The shrouds were lying helpless folded in snow
And the dogs cried out at the passers-by frozen to the bone

He is dead listen The church bell
Sang softly for the death of the sexton
Lise stir up the stove it's going out
The women in the uneasy night were making the
sign of the cross

LA MAISON DES MORTS

à Maurice Raynal

S'étendant sur les côtés du cimetière
La maison des morts l'encadrait comme un cloître
A l'intérieur de ses vitrines
Pareilles à celles des boutiques de modes
Au lieu de sourire debout
Les mannequins grimaçaient pour l'éternité

Arrivé à Munich depuis quinze ou vingt jours
J'étais entré pour la première fois et par hasard
Dans ce cimetière presque désert
Et je claquais des dents
Devant toute cette bourgeoisie
Exposée et vêtue le mieux possible
En attendant la sépulture

Soudain
Rapide comme ma mémoire
Les yeux se rallumèrent
De cellule vitrée en cellule vitrée
Le ciel se peupla d'une apocalypse
Vivace
Et la terre plate à l'infini
Comme avant Galilée
Se couvrit de mille mythologies immobiles
Un ange en diamant brisa toutes les vitrines
Et les morts m'accostèrent
Avec des mines de l'autre monde
Mais leur visage et leurs attitudes
Devinrent bientôt moins funèbres

HOUSE OF THE DEAD

for Maurice Raynal

Stretching along the graveyard's edge
The house of the dead enclosed it like a cloister
Inside its windows
As in boutiques
Mannequins instead of standing up and smiling
Grinned into eternity

Having been in Munich for two or three weeks
I'd come by chance
To the cemetery almost deserted
My teeth on edge
Before so much of the bourgeoisie
All laid out and so well-dressed
Awaiting burial

Suddenly
Like my memory
Their eyes rekindled
From window to window
The sky was filled with an
Apocalypse of life
The earth flat to infinity
As if before the time of Galileo
Was clothed in a thousand fixed mythologies
A diamond angel shattered the windows
And the dead came up to me
With their look of the other world
Their gestures and their faces
Soon became less grave

Le ciel et la terre perdirent
Leur aspect fantasmagorique

Les morts se réjouissaient
De voir leurs corps trépassés entre eux et la lumière
Ils riaient de leur ombre et l'observaient
Comme si véritablement
C'eût été leur vie passée

Alors je les dénombrai
Ils étaient quarante-neuf hommes
Femmes et enfants
Qui embellissaient à vue d'oeil
Et me regardaient maintenant
Avec tant de cordialité
Tant de tendresse même
Que les prenant en amitié
Tout à coup
Je les invitai à une promenade
Loin des arcades de leur maison

Et tous bras dessus bras dessous
Fredonnant des airs militaires
Oui tous vos péchés sont absous
Nous quittâmes le cimitière

Nous traversâmes la ville
Et rencontrions souvent
Des parents des amis qui se joignaient
A la petite troupe des morts récents
Tous étaient si gais

The sky and earth
No more grotesque

The dead rejoiced
To see their bodies
Lying between them and the light
Each watched his shadow laughing
As if it had really
Been his past life

And then I counted
Forty nine men
Women and children
Who visibly before me now
Became more beautiful
And gazed at me
With so much cordiality
And tenderness even
That I took them in friendship
Then and there
Inviting them to go out walking
Far from the archways of their house

Arm in arm
And humming martial airs
Yes yes your sins are all forgiven
We left the cemetery

We crossed the town
Quite often meeting
Friends and family who joined

Si charmants si bien portants
Que bien malin qui aurait pu
Distinguer les morts des vivants

Puis dans la campagne
On s'éparpilla

Deux chevau-légers nous joignirent
On leur fit fête
Ils coupèrent du bois de viorne
Et de sureau
Dont ils firent des sifflets
Qu'ils distribuèrent aux enfants

Plus tard dans un bal champêtre
Les couples mains sur les épaules
Dansèrent au son aigre des cithares

Ils n'avaient pas oublié la danse
Ces morts et ces mortes
On buvait aussi
Et de temps à autre une cloche
Annonçait qu'un nouveau tonneau
Allait être mis en perce

Une morte assise sur un banc
Près d'un buisson d'épine-vinette
Laissait un étudiant
Agenouillé à ses pieds
Lui parler de fiançailles

The little troupe of newly dead
All so lively
All so charming and so healthy
You would have been shrewd
To be able to tell
The living from the dead

Then in the countryside
We scattered

Two cavalrymen who joined us there
Were fêted grandly
And cut down twigs of elder
And viburnum
To carve out whistles
For the children

Later at a country ball
Hands on shoulders the couples danced
To the shrilling of the zithers

They hadn't forgotten
Those dead men and women
How to dance or how to drink
From time to time a bell announced
Another barrel
Would be tapped

A dead girl sitting on a bench
Beside a bush of barberry
Allowed a student

Je vous attendrai
Dix ans vingt ans s'il le faut
Votre volonté sera la mienne

Je vous attendrai
Toute votre vie
Répondait la morte

Des enfants
De ce monde ou bien de l'autre
Chantaient de ces rondes
Aux paroles absurdes et lyriques
Qui sans doute sont les restes

Des plus anciens monuments poétiques
De l'humanité

L'étudiant passa une bague
A l'annulaire de la jeune morte
Voici le gage de mon amour
De nos fiançailles
Ni le temps ni l'absence
Ne nous feront oublier nos promesses
Et un jour nous aurons une belle noce
Des touffes de myrte
A nos vêtements et dans vos cheveux
Un beau sermon à l'église
De longs discours après le banquet
Et de la musique
De la musique

At her feet
To talk to her of marriage

I'll wait ten years
Or even twenty
Your wishes will be mine

I'll wait for you
All through your life
The dead girl answered him

Children
From this world and the other
Sang those rounds
Whose words absurd and lyrical
Are doubtless the remains
Of man's most ancient poems

The student slipped a ring
On his dead girl's wedding finger
This is the symbol of our love
And of our betrothal
Time nor absence
Can make us forget
One day we'll have a beautiful wedding
Sprigs of myrtle
On our clothes and in your hair
A fine sermon in church
Long speeches after the banquet
And music
Music

Nos enfants
Dit la fiancée
Seront plus beaux plus beaux encore
Hélas! la bague était brisée
Que s'ils étaient d'argent ou d'or
D'émeraude ou de diamant
Seront plus clairs plus clairs encore
Que les astres du firmament
Que la lumière de l'aurore
Que vos regards mon fiancé
Auront meilleure odeur encore
Hélas! la bague était brisée
Que le lilas qui vient d'éclore
Que le thym la rose ou qu'un brin
De lavande ou de romarin

Les musiciens s'en étant allés
Nous continuâmes la promenade

Au bord d'un lac

On s'amusa à faire des ricochets
Avec des cailloux plats
Sur l'eau qui dansait à peine

Des barques étaient amarrées
Dans un havre
On les détacha
Après que toute la troupe se fut embarquée
Et quelques morts ramaient
Avec autant de vigueur que les vivants

Our children
Said the fiancée
Will be more beautiful
Alas! the ring was broken
More beautiful than gold or silver
Emerald or diamond
Clearer than the dawn's first light
Than stars in the firmament
Clearer than your eyes my love
More fragrant than
Alas! the ring was broken
Than lilacs newly bloomed
Than roses thyme or a s;prig
Of lavender or rosemary

The musicians had gone
We went on our way

At the edges of a lake
We amused ourselves
Skidding flat pebbles
On water which hardly moved

Some boats were moored
In a harbour
Untying them
We all embarked
Some of the dead rowed just as
Strongly as the living

A l'avant du bateau que je gouvernais
Un mort parlait avec une jeune femme
Vêtue d'une robe jaune
D'un corsage noir
Avec des rubans bleus et d'un chapeau gris
Orné d'une seule petite plume défrisée

Je vous aime
Disait-il
Comme le pigeon aime la colombe
Comme l'insecte nocturne
Aime la lumière

Trop tard
Répondait la vivante
Repoussez repoussez cet amour défendu
Je suis mariée
Voyez l'anneau qui brille
Mes mains tremblent
Je pleure et je voudrais mourir

Les barques étaient arrivées
A un endroit ou les chevau-légers
Savaient qu'un écho répondait de la rive
On ne se laissait point de l'interroger

Il y eut des questions si extravagantes
Et des réponses tellement pleines d'à-propos
Que c'était à mourir de rire
Et le mort disait à la vivante

In the bow of the boat which I was steering
A dead man was speaking with a young woman
Dressed in a yellow gown
Her bodice black with blue ribbons
A grey hat with an uncurled feather

I love you
He said
As the pigeon loves the dove
As the insect at night
Is in love with the light

Too late
Answered the living woman
Deny deny that forbidden love
I am a wife
See the wedding ring which shines
My hands are trembling
I'm weeping and would like to die

The boats pulled in
Where the cavalrymen
Knew that the bank would give an echo
Tirelessly we asked our questions
Questions so extravagant
And then such witty answers
We could have died of laughter
And the dead man said to the living woman

Nous serions si heureux ensemble
Sur nous l'eau se refermera
Mais vous pleurez et vos mains tremblent
Aucun de nous ne reviendra

On reprit terre et ce fut le retour
Les amoureux s'entr'aimaient
Et par couples aux belles bouches
Marchaient à distances inégales
Les morts avaient choisi les vivantes
Et les vivants
Des mortes
Un genévrier parfois
Faisait l'effet d'un fantôme
Les enfants déchiraient l'air
En soufflant les joues creuses
Dans leurs sifflets de viorne
Ou de sureau
Tandis que les militaires
Chantaient des tyroliennes
En se répondant comme on le fait
Dans la montagne

Dans la ville
Notre troupe diminua peu à peu
On se disait
Au revoir
A demain
A bientôt
Beaucoup entraient dans les brasseries
Quelques-uns nous quittèrent

How happy we would be together
The water will close back over us
You're weeping and your hands are trembling
None of us will be returning

We landed again and set off homewards
The courting lovers
With beautiful mouths
Walking at different distances
Dead men had chosen living women
And the living men
Dead women
A juniper sometimes
Would seem a ghost
Children split the air
Blowing with their hollow cheeks
Whistles of elder
Or viburnum
While soldiers sang
Their Tyrolean songs
Calling responses
As if on the mountains

In the town
Our troupe diminished bit by bit
Saying goodbyes
And see you soons
Quite a few went into bars
Some left at the dog-butcher's
To buy the evening meal

Devant une boucherie canine
Pour y acheter leur repas du soir

Bientôt je restai seul avec ces morts
Qui s'en allaient tout droit
Au cimetière
Où
Sous les Arcades
Je les reconnus
Couchés
Immobiles
Et bien vêtus
Attendant la sépulture derrière les vitrines

Ils ne se doutaient pas
De ce qui s'était passé
Mais les vivants en gardaient le souvenir
C'était un bonheur inespéré
Et si certain
Qu'ils ne craignaient point de la perdre

Soon I alone was left with the dead
Who were going straight on
To the graveyard
Where
Under the arches
I saw them again
Lying stiffly
And so well-dressed
Inside the glass
Awaiting burial

They had no suspicion
Of what had happened
But the living held on to the memory
A happiness so unhoped for
And so sure
They did not fear its loss

Ils vivaient si noblement
Que ceux qui la veille encore
Les regardaient comme leurs égaux
Ou même quelque chose de moins
Admiraient maintenant
Leur puissance leur richesse et leur génie
Car y a-t-il rien qui vous élève
Comme d'avoir aimé un mort ou une morte
On devient si pur qu'on en arrive
Dans les glaciers de la mémoire
A se confondre avec le souvenir
On est fortifié pour la vie
Et l'on n'a plus besoin de personne

They lived so nobly
That those who just the night before
Had seen them as their equals
Or maybe something less
Admired them now
Their strength their richness and their spirit
For is there anything more uplifting
Than love for a dead man or woman
You become so pure that you end up
In the glaciers of remembrance
Mistaking yourself for the memory
And strengthened thus for life
No longer in need of anyone

SCHINDERHANNES

à Marius-Ary Leblond

Dans la forêt avec sa bande
Schinderhannes s'est désarmé
Le brigand près de sa brigande
Hennit d'amour au joli mai

Benzel accroupi lit la Bible
Sans voir que son chapeau pointu
A plume d'aigle sert de cible
A Jacob Born le mal foutu

Juliette Blaesius qui rote
Fait semblant d'avoir le hoquet
Hannes pousse une fausse note
Quand Schulz vient portant un baquet

Et s'écrie en versant des larmes
Baquet plein de vin parfumé
Viennent aujourd'hui les gendarmes
Nous aurons bu le vin de mai

Allons Julia la mam'zelle
Bois avec nous ce clair bouillon
D'herbes et de vin de Moselle
Prosit Bandit en cotillon

SCHINDERHANNES

for Marius-Ary Leblond

In the forest with his gang
Schinderhannes lays down his weapons
The brigand with his brigandess
Trumpets his love across the May

Benzel squatting reads his Bible
Not seeing that his pointed hat
With eagle plume presents a target
For Jacob Born the crippled one

Juliette Blaesius who burps
Makes as if she's got the hiccups
When Schulz comes carrying a bucket
Hannes lands on a flattened note

Intoning while he starts to cry
O bucket full of scented wine
Who cares if police come by today
We will have drunk the wine of May

Come now Julia my girl
Try with us this bouillon
Of herbs and Moselle wine
Here's to the brigand in her skirts

Cette brigande est bientôt soûle
Et veut Hannes qui n'en veut pas
Pas d'amour maintenant ma poule
Sers-nous un bon petit repas

Il faut ce soir que j'assassine
Ce riche juif au bord du Rhin
Au clair des torches de résine
La fleur de mai c'est le florin

On mange alors toute la bande
Pète et rit pendant le dîner
Puis s'attendrit à l'allemande
Avant d'aller assassiner

The brigandess is soon quite drunk
And wanting Hannes who doesn't want her
No time for loving now my pet
What we need's a meal

Tonight down by the river's edge
By the light of these resin torches
I must kill a rich Jew
The flower of May is a florin

And so the gang eat
While farting and laughing
Then soften a little as Germans will
Before going out to kill

LA SYNAGOGUE

Ottomar Scholem et Abraham Loeweren
Coiffés de feutres verts le matin du sabbat
Vont à la synagogue en longeant le Rhin
Et les coteaux où les vignes rougissent là-bas

Ils se disputent et crient des choses qu'on ose
à peine traduire
Bâtard conçu pendant les règles ou Que le diable
entre dans ton père
Le vieux Rhin soulève sa face ruisselante et se détourne
pour sourire
Ottomar Scholem et Abraham Loeweren sont en colère

Parce que pendant le sabbat on ne doit pas fumer
Tandis que les chrétiens passent avec des cigares allumés
Et parce qu'Ottomar et Abraham aiment tous deux
Lia aux yeux de brebis et dont le ventre avance un peu

Pourtant tout à l'heure dans la synagogue l'un après l'autre
Ils baiseront la thora en soulevant leur beau chapeau
Parmi les feuillards de la fête des cabanes
Ottomar en chantant sourira à Abraham

Ils déchanteront sans mesure et les voix graves des hommes
Feront gémir un Léviathan au fond du Rhin comme
une voix d'automne
Et dans la synagogue pleine de chapeaux on agitera
les loulabim
Hanoten ne Kamoth bagoim tholahoth baleoumim

THE SYNAGOGUE

Ottomar Scholem and Abraham Loeweren
Wearing green hats on the sabbath morning
Walk to the synagogue alongside the Rhine
And the slopes where the vines are reddening

They argue and shout what one shouldn't translate
Bastard got during a period May the devil take hold of
your father
The old Rhine lifts his dripping face and turns aside
to smile
Ottomar Scholem and Abraham Loeweren are angry because

On the day of the sabbath one may not smoke
Yet Christians go by with lighted cigars
And also because they both love Lia
Lia of the lamb-like eyes whose belly is advanced a little

Soon in the synagogue each in turn
Will be kissing the Torah and lifting fine hats
Surounded by boughs of the feast of cabins
Ottomar singing will smile at Abraham

In the deep voice of men they will chant out of time
And make a whale groan like the voice of autumn
far down in the Rhine
And in the synagogue filled with hats they'll wave
the loulabim
Hanoten ne Kamoth bagoim tholahoth baleoumim

LES CLOCHES

Mon beau tzigane mon amant
Écoute les cloches qui sonnent
Nous nous aimions éperdument
Croyant n'être vus de personne

Mais nous étions bien mal cachés
Toutes les cloches à la ronde
Nous ont vus du haut des clochers
Et le disent à tout le monde

Demain Cyprien et Henri
Marie Ursule et Catherine
La boulangère et son mari
Et puis Gertrude ma cousine

Souriront quand je passerai
Je ne saurai plus où me mettre
Tu sera loin Je pleurerai
J'en mourrai peut-être

THE BELLS

Listen there my handsome gypsy
Listen to the bells that ring
Alone we made our love and madly
Thinking to be seen by no one

But we were very poorly hidden
The bells all round
Had seen us from their steeples
And spread it to the world

Tomorrow Cyprien and Henri
Marie Ursule and Catherine
The baker's wife her husband too
And then Gertrude my cousin

Will smile as I go by
I won't know where to hide myself
You'll be gone and I'll be crying
                    I'll die of it maybe

SALTIMBANQUES

à Louis Dumur

Dans la plaine les baladins
S'éloignent au long des jardins
Devant l'huis des auberges grises
Par les villages sans églises

Et les enfants s'en vont devant
Les autres suivent en rêvant
Chaque arbre fruitier se résigne
Quand de très loin ils lui font signe

Ils ont des poids ronds ou carrés
Des tambours des cerceaux dorés
L'ours et le singe animaux sages
Quêtent des sous sur leur passage

JESTERS

for Louis Dumur

Across the plain the strolling players
Slip by the gardens
The doors of grey inns
And villages without a church

The children go on out in front
The others follow dreaming
Each fruit tree resigns itself
When pointed at in the distance

They carry weights both round and square
Drums and golden hoops
The monkey and the bear wise beasts
Beg pennies passing through

CRÉPUSCULE

à Mademoiselle Marie Laurencin

Frôlée par les ombres des morts
Sur l'herbe où le jour s'exténue
L'arlequine s'est mise nue
Et dans l'étang mire son corps

Un charlatan crépusculaire
Vante les tours que l'on va faire
Le ciel sans teinte est constellé
D'astres pâles comme du lait

Sur les tréteaux l'arlequin blême
Salue d'abord les spectatuers
Des sorciers venus de Bohême
Quelques fées et les enchanteurs

Ayant décroché une étoile
Il la manie à bras tendu
Tandis que les pieds un pendu
Sonne en mesure les cymbales

L'aveugle berce un bel enfant
La biche passe avec ses faons
Le nain regarde d'un air triste
Grandir l'arlequin trismégiste

TWILIGHT

for Miss Marie Laurencin

Brushed by the shadows of the dead
On the grass where the day is ending
Columbine takes off her clothes
And in the pool admires her body

A charlatan of twilight
Boasts of the tricks he is going to do
The sky without colour
Is set with stars as pale as milk

On the boards the ghostly harlequin
Salutes his audience
Sorcerers from Bohemia
Fairies and magicians

Then unfastening a star
He wields it at arm's length
While from the feet of a dangling man
Cymbals clash in time

The blind man nurses a beautiful child
The doe goes by with her fawns
The harlequin grows three times bigger
The dwarf is sadly looking on

UN FANTÔME DE NUÉES

Comme c'était la veille du quatorze juillet
Vers les quatre heures de l'après-midi
Je descendis dans la rue pour aller voir les saltimbanques

Ces gens qui font des tours en plein air
Commencent à être rares à Paris
Dans ma jeunesse on en voyait beaucoup plus
        qu'aujourd'hui
Ils s'en sont allés presque tous en province

Je pris le boulevard Saint-Germain
Et sur une petite place située entre Saint-Germain-
        des-Prés et la statue de Danton
Je rencontrai les saltimbanques

La foule les entourait muette et résignée à attendre
Je me fis une place dans ce cercle afin de tout voir
Poids formidables
Villes de Belgique soulevées à bras tendu par
        un ouvrier russe de Longwy
Haltères noirs et creux qui ont pour tige un fleuve figé
Doigts roulant une cigarette amère et délicieuse comme
        la vie

De nombreux tapis sales couvraient le sol
Tapis qui ont des plis qu'on ne défera pas
Tapis qui sont presque entièrement couleur de la poussière
Et où quelques taches jaunes ou vertes ont persisté
Comme un air de musique qui vous poursuit

PHANTOM OF CLOUDS

As it was the eve of 14 July
Towards four in the afternoon
I went down to the street to see the clowns

These folk who perform in the open air
Are starting to be rare in Paris
In my youth one saw them much more than today
They've almost entirely gone to the provinces

I took the Boulevard Saint-Germain
And in a little square between Saint-Germain-des-Prés
and the statue of Danton
I met the clowns

The crowd around them was quiet and patient
I found a place in the circle to see everything
Formidable weights
Belgian towns raised by the outstretched arms of a Russian
workman from Longwy
Black and hollow dumb-bells a solid river for a shaft
Fingers rolling a cigarette delicious and bitter as life

Some dirty carpets covered the ground
Carpets with folds that won't rub out
Carpets almost
the colour of dust
Where several green or yellow spots persist
Like a tune you can't shake off

Vois-tu le personnage maigre et sauvage
La cendre de ses pères lui sortait en barbe grisonnante
Il portait ainsi toute son hérédité au visage
Il semblait rêver à l'avenir
En tournant machinalement un orgue de Barbarie
Dont la lente voix se lamentait merveilleusement
Les glousglous les couacs et les sourds gémissements

Les saltimbanques ne bougeaient pas
Le plus vieux avait un maillot couleur de ce rose
violâtre qu'ont aux joues certaines jeunes
filles fraîches mais près de la mort

Ce rose-là se niche surtout dans les plis qui entourent
souvent leur bouche
Ou près des narines
C'est un rose plein de traîtrise

Cet homme portait-il ainsi sur le dos
La teinte ignoble de ses poumons

Les bras les bras partout montaient la garde

Le second saltimbanque
N'était vêtu que de son ombre
Je le regardai longtemps
Son visage m'échappe entièrement
C'est un homme sans tête

Do you see that fellow wild and thin
The ashes of his fathers greying in his beard
His heritage entirely in his face
He seemed to be dreaming of the future
As he turned mechanically a Barbary organ
Whose slow voice was moaning marvellously
In gurgles squawks and muffled groans

The clowns did not move
The oldest had tights the colour of that violet rose which
    certain girls develop in their cheeks when
    young but close to death

That violet rose which is found so often in wrinkles which
    surround the mouth
Or near the nostrils
A rose full of treachery

The man thus wore upon his back
The wretched colour of his lungs

The arms the arms were everywhere on guard

The second clown
Wore nothing but his shadow
I stared at him a long while
His face escapes me completely
He is a man without a head

Un autre enfin avait l'air d'un voyou
D'un apache bon et crapule à la fois
Avec son pantalon bouffant et les accroche-chaussettes
N'aurait-il pas eu l'apparence d'un maquereau à sa toilette

La musique se tut et ce furent des pourparlers avec
le public
Qui sou à sou jeta sur le tapis la somme de deux francs
cinquante
Au lieu des trois francs que le vieux avait fixés comme
prix des tours

Mais quand il fut clair que personne ne donnerait plus rien
On se décida à commencer la séance
De dessous l'orgue sortit un tout petit saltimbanque
habillé de rose pulmonaire
Avec de la fourrure aux poignets et aux chevilles
Il poussait des cris brefs
Et saluait en écartant gentiment les avant-bras
Mains ouvertes

Une jambe en arrière prête à la génuflexion
Il salua ainsi aux quatre points cardinaux

Et quand il marcha sur une boule
Son corps mince devint une musique si délicate que nul
parmi les spectateurs n'y fut insensible
Un petit esprit sans aucune humanité
Pensa chacun
Et cette musique des formes
Détruisit celle de l'orgue mécanique
Que moulait l'homme au visage couvert d'ancêtres

Another indeed had a ruffian air
A genuine gangster seedy but pure
His baggy trousers and gartered socks
Wouldn't he look like a preening pimp

The music stopped they parleyed with the crowd
Who sou by sou threw down on the mat the sum of
two francs fifty
Instead of the three which the old man had fixed as the
price of performance

But when it was clear that no one would give any more
They decided to get under way
From under the organ a tiny clown came dressed in
pulmonary pink
With fur on his ankles and on his wrists

He called out sharply and bowed
Parting his forearms gently
Open-handed

One leg behind as if to genuflect
He saluted the four points of the compass
And when he walked on a ball
His thin body became such a delicate music that no one
watching could fail to be moved
A little soul without humanity
Each thought to himself
And this music of forms
Destroyed what was ground from the barrel organ
By the man whose face was bearded with ancestors

Le petit saltimbanque fit la roue
Avec tant d'harmonie
Que l'orgue cessa de jouer
Et que l'organiste se cacha le visage dans les mains
Aux doigts semblables aux descendants de son destin
Foetus minuscules qui lui sortaient de la barbe
Nouveaux cris de Peau-Rouge
Musique angèlique des arbres
Disparition de l'enfant
Les saltimbanques soulevèrent les gros haltères à bout
de bras
Ils jonglèrent avec les poids

Mais chaque spectateur cherchait en soi l'enfant miraculeux
Siècle ô siècle des nuages

The little clown did cartwheels
With so much harmony
The organ ceased
And the organist buried his face in hands
Which looked like his fated descendants
Minuscule foetuses came from his beard
Horrific screams
Angelic music from the trees
Disappearance of the child
The clowns with their arms took up their huge dumb-bells
They juggled with weights

But each one in the crowd was seeking in himself the
miraculous child
Century o century of clouds

MARIZIBILL

Dans la Haute-Rue à Cologne
Elle allait et venait le soir
Offerte à tous en tout mignonne
Puis buvait lasse des trottoirs
Très tard dans les brasseries borgnes

Elle se mettait sur la paille
Pour un maqueraux roux et rose
C'était un juif il sentait l'ail
Et l'avait venant de Formose
Tirée d'un bordel de Changaï

Je connais gens de toutes sortes
Ils n'égalent pas leurs destins
Indécise comme feuilles mortes
Leurs yeux sont de feux mal éteints
Leurs coeurs bougent comme leurs portes

MARIZIBILL

Along the High Street of Cologne
She came and went each evening
Soliciting sweetly all who passed
Then weary of the streets went drinking
All night in decrepit bars

She ruined herself
For a red-headed pimp
A pink-faced Jew who smelt of garlic
Who on a trip home from Formosa
Took her from a Shanghai brothel

People of all sorts I've known
Unequal to their fates
Irresolute as fallen leaves
Their eyes like half-extinguished fires
Their hearts swing open like their doors

LA PORTE

La porte de l'hôtel sourit terriblement
Qu'est-ce que cela peut me faire ô ma maman
D'être cet employé pour qui seul rien n'existe
Pi-mus couples allant dans la profonde eau triste
Anges frais débarqués à Marseille hier matin
J'entends mourir et remourir un chant lointain
Humble comme je suis qui ne suis rien qui vaille

Enfant je t'ai donné ce que j'avais travaille

THE DOOR

The hotel door smiles terribly
Oh mama what will it do to me
To be that clerk for whom alone
Nothing can exist
Fish swim coupled through deep sad water
Fresh angels disembarked at Marseilles yesterday
I hear a distant song dying and dying again
I who am humble and worth nothing

Child I gave you what I had now work

ANNIE

Sur la côte du Texas
Entre Mobile et Galveston il y a
Un grand jardin tout plein de roses
Il contient aussi une villa
Qui est une grande rose

Une femme se promène souvent
Dans le jardin toute seule
Et quand je passe sur la route bordée de tilleuls
Nous nous regardons

Comme cette femme est mennonite
Ses rosiers et ses vêtements n'ont pas de boutons
Il en manque deux à mon veston
La dame et moi suivons presque le même rite

ANNIE

On the coast of Texas
Between Mobile and Galveston
There is a huge garden filled with roses
And a villa which is
One great rose

A woman is often walking there
Out in the garden all alone
When I walk by on the lime tree road
We see each other passing

She is a Mennonite and so
Her rose-trees and her clothes
Do not have buttons
From my jacket two are missing
Our ritual's the same almost

HÔTELS

La chambre est veuve
Chacun pour soi
Présence neuve
On paye au mois

Le patron doute
Payera-t-on
Je tourne en route
Comme un toton

Le bruit des fiacres
Mon voisin laid
Qui fume un âcre
Tabac anglais

O La Vallière
Qui boite et rit
De mes prières
Table de nuit

Et tous ensemble
Dans cet hôtel
Savons la langue
Comme à Babel

Fermons nos portes
A double tour
Chacun apporte
Son seul amour

HOTELS

The room is widowed
Each to himself
A new guest now
And payments monthly

The landlord doubts
If he'll be paid
I pass him by
Like a turning top

The noise of cabs
My ugly neighbour
Smokes a vile
Tabac anglais

O La Vallière
Limping and laughing
At my prayers
O bedside table

And all together
In this hotel
We find the tongue
They used in Babel

Lock up your doors
With a double turn
Each man bears
His love alone

LA BLANCHE NEIGE

Les anges les anges dans le ciel
L'un est vêtu en officier
L'un est vêtu en cuisinier
Et les autres chantent

Bel officier couleur du ciel
Le doux printemps longtemps après Noël
Te médaillera d'un beau soleil
                    D'un beau soleil

Le cuisinier plume les oies
                    Ah! tombe neige
                    Tombe et que n'ai-je
Ma bien-aimée entre mes bras

WHITE SNOW

Angels angels in the sky
One dressed as an officer
One as a cook
The others are singing

Handsome officer colour of sky
Sweet spring a long time after Christmas
Will give you a medal
The beautiful sun

The cook strips feathers from the geese
Ah let the snow come down
Let it fall and let me have
My loved one in my arms

CORS DE CHASSE

Notre histoire est noble et tragique
Comme le masque d'un tyran
Nul drame hasardeux ou magique
Aucun détail indifférent
Ne rend notre amour pathétique

Et Thomas de Quincey buvant
L'opium poison doux et chaste
A sa pauvre Anne allait rêvant
Passons passons puisque tout passe
Je me retournerai souvent

Les souvenirs sont cors de chasse
Dont meurt le bruit parmi le vent

HUNTING HORNS

Our story is noble and tragic
A kind of tyrant's masque
No drama of chance or magic
No detail unremarked
Makes pathos of our love

And Thomas de Quincey taking
Pure poison from a glass
To his poor Anne went dreaming
Since all is passing we too pass
I'll be remembering still

Memories are hunting horns
Dying in the wind

de LES FIANÇAILLES

J'ai le courage de regarder en arrière
Les cadavres de mes jours
Marquent ma route et je les pleure
Les uns pourrissent dans les églises italiennes
Ou bien dans de petits bois de citronniers
Qui fleurissent et fructifient
En même temps et en toute saison
D'autres jours ont pleuré avant de mourir dans
des tavernes
Où d'ardents bouquets rouaient
Aux yeux d'une mulâtresse qui inventait la poésie
Et les roses de l'électricité s'ouvrent encore
Dans le jardin de ma mémoire

From THE BETROTHAL

I have had the courage to look back
The corpses of my days
Mark off my journey and I mourn them
Some rot in Italian churches
Or in the little lemon groves
Which flower and bear fruit
At once and in all seasons
Other days wept before dying in taverns
Where bouquets flared
In the eyes of a mulatto girl inventing poetry
And the roses of electricity are blooming still
In the garden of my memory

INSCRIPTION POUR LE TOMBEAU DU PEINTRE HENRI ROUSSEAU DOUANIER

Gentil Rousseau tu nous entends
Nous te saluons
Delaunay sa femme Monsieur Queval et moi
Laisse passer nos bagages en franchise à la porte du ciel
Nous t'apporterons des pinceaux des couleurs des toiles
Afin que tes loisirs sacrés dans la lumière réelle
Tu les consacres à peindre comme tu tiras mon portrait
La face des étoiles

INSCRIPTION FOR THE TOMB OF THE PAINTER HENRI ROUSSEAU DOUANIER

Gentle Rousseau you can hear us
We greet you
Delaunay his wife Monsieur Queval and I
Let our luggage duty-free through heaven's gate
We're bringing brushes paints and canvas
So you can give your sacred hours
To painting in the light eternal
Just as once you made my portrait
The face of the stars

SOUVENIR DU DOUANIER

Un tout petit oiseau
Sur l'épaule d'un ange
Ils chantent la louange
Du gentil Rousseau

Les mouvements du monde
Les souvenirs s'en vont
Comme un bateau sur l'onde
Et les regrets au fond

Gentil Rousseau
Tu es cet ange
Et cet oiseau
De ta louange

Ils se dormaient la main et s'attristaient ensemble
Sur leurs tombeaux ce sont les mêmes fleurs qui tremblent
Tu as raison elle est belle

Mais je n'ai pas le droit de l'aimer
Il faut que je reste ici
Où l'on fait de si jolies couronnes mortuaires en perles
Il faudra que je te montre ça

La belle Américaine
Qui rend les hommes fous
Dans deux ou trois semaines
Partira pour Corfou

MEMORIES OF THE DOUANIER

The smallest of birds
On an angel's shoulder
They sing in salute
Of the gentle Rousseau

Moods of the world
And memories pass
Like a boat on the sea
And the deepest of griefs

Gentle Rousseau
You are the angel
You are the bird
To sing your own praise

Hands linked they were growing sad together
On their tombs tremble identical flowers
You are right she is beautiful

But I do not have the right to love her
I must stay here
Where they make such pretty wreaths in pearl
I will have to show you that

The American beauty
Who drives men mad
In two or three weeks
Will leave for Corfu

Je tourne vire
Phare affolé
Mon beau navire
S'est en allé

Des plaies sur les jambes
Tu m'as montré ces trous sanglants
Quand nous prenions un quinquina
Au bar des Iles Marquises rue de la Gaîté
Un matin doux de verduresse

Les matelots l'attendent
Et fixent l'horizon
Où mi-corps hors de l'onde
Bayent tous les poissons

Je tourne vire
Phare affolé
Mon beau navire
S'est en allé

Les tessons de la voix que l'amour a brisée
Nègres mélodieux Et je t'avais grisée

La belle Américaine
Qui rend les hommes fous
Dans deux ou trois semaines
Partira pour Corfou

Tu traverses Paris à pied très lentement
La brise au voile mauve Etes-vous là maman

I turn and veer
A lighthouse crazed
My beautiful ship
Has gone away

Gashes on the legs
You've shown me grievous wounds
As we took a quinquina
At the bar des Iles Marquises on the rue de la Gaîté
A soft morning of green

The sailors look out
And scan the horizon
Where half out of the water
The fish gape in air

I turn and veer
A lighthouse crazed
My beautiful ship
Has gone away

The splinters of your voice that love has broken
Melodious negroes And I had got you high

The American beauty
Who drives men mad
In two or three weeks
Will leave for Corfu

You walk across Paris on very slow feet
A breeze in the mauve veil That you mama

Je tourne vire
Phare affolé
Mon beau navire
S'est en allé

On dit qu'elle était belle
Près du Mississippi
Mais que la rend plus belle
La mode de Paris

Je tourne vire
Phare affolé
Mon beau navire
S'est en allé

Il grava sur un banc près de la porte Dauphine
Les deux noms adorés Clémence et Joséphine

Et deux rosiers grimpaient le long de son âme
Un merveilleux trio
Il sourit sur le Pavé des Gardes à la jument pisseuse
Il dirige un orchestre d'enfants
Mademoiselle Madeleine
Ah! Mademoiselle Madeleine
Ah!

Il y a d'autres filles
Dans l'arrondissement
De douces de gentilles
Et qui n'ont pas d'amants

I turn and veer
A lighthouse crazed
My beautiful ship
Has gone away

They say she was fine
By the Mississippi
But the fashions of Paris
Have given her style

I turn and veer
A lighthouse crazed
My beautiful ship
Has gone away

He carved once on a bench by the Porte Dauphine
His two loved names Clémence and Joséphine

And two wild roses climbed along his soul
A marvellous trio
On the Pavé des Gardes he smiles at the pissing mare
And leads an orchestra of children
Mademoiselle Madeleine
Ah! Mademoiselle Madeleine
Ah!

In the quarter
There are other girls
Pliant and soft ones
Who do not have lovers

Je tourne vire
Phare affolé
Mon beau navire
S'est en allé

I turn and veer
A lighthouse crazed
My beautiful ship
Has gone away

FÊTE

A André Rouveyre

Feu d'artifice en acier
Qu'il est charmant cet éclairage
Artifice d'artificier
Mêler quelque grâce au courage

Deux fusants
Rose éclatement
Comme deux seins que l'on dégrafe
Tendent leurs bouts insolemment
IL SUT AIMER
quelle épitaphe

Un poète dans la forêt
Regarde avec indifférence
Son revolver au cran d'arrêt
Des roses mourir d'espérance

Il songe aux roses de Saadi
Et soudain sa tête se penche
Car une rose lui redit
La molle courbe d'une hanche

L'air est plein d'un terrible alcool
Filtré des étoiles mi-closes
Les obus caressent le mol
Parfum nocturne où tu reposes
Mortification des roses

FESTIVAL

To André Rouveyre

Fireworks of steel
What a charming display
What cunning of the fireworker
To mix such grace with courage

Two shells
Pink bursts
Like two uncovered breasts
Insolently hold out their points
HE KNEW HOW TO LOVE
                    Now there's an epitaph

A poet in the forest
Looks indifferently upon
          His revolver on safe
And the roses dying of hope

He is thinking of the Saadi roses
And suddenly he bends down his head
As a rose brings back again
The soft curve of a hip

The air is filled with a terrible liquor
Filtering through half-closed stars
The shells are caressing the soft
Night perfume where you rest
                    Humiliation of roses

LE DÉPART

Et leurs visages étaient pâles
Et leurs sanglots s'étaient brisés

Comme la neige aux purs pétales
Ou bien tes mains sur mes baisers
Tombaient les feuilles automnales

THE DEPARTURE

And their faces were pale
And their sobs were broken

As if pure petals of the snow
Or your hands upon my kisses
The autumn leaves were falling

L'ADIEU DU CAVALIER

Ah Dieu! que la guerre est jolie
Avec ses chants ses longs loisirs
Cette bague je l'ai polie
Le vent se mêle à vos soupirs

Adieu! voici le boute-selle
Il disparut dans un tournant
Et mourut là-bas tandis qu'elle
Riait au destin surprenant

L'ADIEU DU CAVALIER

Ah God! how fine the war is
With its songs its long hours of leisure
That ring how I have made it shine
The wind is mingled with your sighs

Farewell! here is the boot and saddle
He vanished round a bend
And died just over there while she
Laughed at the ways of destiny

EXERCICE

Vers un village de l'arrière
S'en allaient quatre bombardiers
Ils étaient couverts de poussière
Depuis la tête jusqu'aux pieds

Ils regardaient la vaste plaine
En parlant entre eux du passé
Et ne se retournaient qu'à peine
Quand un obus avait toussé

Tout quatre de la classe seize
Parlaient d'antan non d'avenir
Ainsi se prolongeait l'ascèse
Qui les exerçait à mourir

EXERCISE

Towards a village in the rear
Four bombardiers were walking
Dressed in dust
From head to toe

Looking out across the plain
They talked together of the past
And when a shell had coughed
They'd hardly bother turning

All four of the '16 class
Spoke not of the future but of the past
Extending thus the programme
Which trained them to die

LES SAISONS

C'était un temps béni nous étions sur les plages
Va-t'en de bon matin pieds nus et sans chapeau
Et vite comme va la langue d'un crapaud
L'amour blessait au coeur les fous comme les sages

As-tu connu Guy au galop
Du temps qu'il était militaire
As-tu connu Guy au galop
Du temps qu'il était artiflot
A la guerre

C'était un temps béni Le temps du vaguemestre
On est bien plus serré que dans les autobus
Et des astres passaient qui singeaient les obus
Quand dans la nuit survint la batterie équestre

As-tu connu Guy au galop
Du temps qu'il était militaire
As-tu connu Guy au galop
Du temps qu'il était artiflot
A la guerre

C'était un temps béni Jours vagues et nuits vagues
Les marmites donnaient aux rondins des cagnats
Quelque aluminium où tu t'ingénias
A limer jusqu'au soir d'invraisemblables bagues

THE SEASONS

A blessed time it was on the beaches
Barefoot from early morning and without hats
And quickly as a toad sticks out its tongue
Love struck at the hearts of wise men and clowns

Do you remember galloping Guy
When he was in the army
Do you remember Guy at the gallop
Who joined the artillery
Up the the front

It was a blessed time Season of the baggage-master
Packed in tighter than a bus
And shells would ape the passing stars
As the cavalry came from the dark

Do you remember galloping Guy
When he was in the army
Do you remember Guy at the gallop
Who joined the artillery
Up the the front

It was a blessed time Uncertain days uncertain nights
Where shells dropped in the logs of dug-outs
Bits of aluminium which you
Would file until dusk to improbable rings

As-tu connu Guy au galop
Du temps qu'il était militaire
As-tu connu Guy au galop
Du temps qu'il était artiflot
A la guerre

C'était un temps béni La guerre continue
Les Servants ont limé la bague au long des mois
Le Conducteur écoute abrité dans les bois
La chanson que répète une étoile inconnue

As-tu connu Guy au galop
Du temps qu'il était militaire
As-tu connu Guy au galop
Du temps qu'il était artiflot
A la guerre

Do you remember galloping Guy
When he was in the army
Do you remember Guy at the gallop
Who joined the artillery
Up the the front

It was a blessed time The war goes on
The gunners for months have been filing the ring
Out in the woods the leader hears
The song given back by an unknown star

Do you remember galloping Guy
When he was in the army
Do you remember Guy at the gallop
Who joined the artillery
Up the the front

TOURBILLON DES MOUCHES

Un cavalier va dans la plaine
La jeune fille pense à lui
Et cette flotte à Mytilène
Le fil de fer est là qui luit

Comme ils cueillaient la rose ardente
Leurs yeux tout à coup ont fleuri
Mais quel soleil la bouche errante
A qui la bouche avait souri

WHIRLWIND OF FLIES

A horseman goes across the plain
A young girl thinks of him
And that fleet at Mytilene
The wire still gleaming there

As they were picking the eager rose
Their eyes quite suddenly bloomed
What sun now for the straying mouth
At which a mouth had smiled

OMBRE

Vous voilà de nouveau près de moi
Souvenirs de mes compagnons morts à la guerre
L'olive du temps
Souvenirs qui n'en faites plus d'un
Comme cent fourrures ne font qu'un manteau
Comme ces milliers de blessures ne font qu'un article
de journal
Apparence impalpable et sombre qui avez pris
La forme changeante de mon ombre
Un Indien à l'affût pendant l'éternité
Ombre vous rampez près de moi
Mais vous ne m'entendez plus
Vous ne connaîtrez plus les poèmes divins que je chante
Tandis que moi je vous entends je vous vois encore
Destinés
Ombre multiple que le soleil vous garde
Vous qui m'aimez assez pour ne jamais me quitter
Et qui dansez au soleil sans faire de poussière
Ombre encre du soleil
Écriture de ma lumière
Caisson de regrets
Un dieu qui s'humilie

SHADOW

There you are once more beside me
Memories of my friends dead in the war
Olive of the season
Memories which make no more than one
As a hundred furs will make a single coat
As a thousand wounds will make one journalist's report
Phantom intangible and dark you who have taken
My shadow's changing shape
An Indian in wait through all eternity
You crawl beside me ghost
But you do not hear me anymore
You'll not know of these exalted poems that I sing
Although I hear and see you still
Doomed
Myriad ghost may the sun protect you
You who so love me that you cannot leave
Who dance in the sun without making dust
Ink shadow of the sun
Writing of my light
Caisson of regrets
A god who stoops

GUERRE

Rameau central de combat
Contact par l'écoute
On tire dans la direction 'des bruits entendus'
Les jeunes de la classe 1915
Et ces fils de fer électrisés
Ne pleurez donc pas sur les horreurs de la guerre
Avant elle nous n'avions que la surface
De la terre et des mers
Après elle nous aurons les abîmes
Le sous-sol et l'espace aviatique
Maîtres du timon
Après après
Nous prendrons toutes les joies
Des vainqueurs qui se délassent
Femmes Jeux Usines Commerce
Industrie Agriculture Métal
Feu Cristal Vitesse
Voix Regard Tact à part
Et ensemble dans le tact venu de loin
De plus loin encore
De l'Au-delà de cette terre

WAR

Main line of battle
Contact by listening-post
Fire in direction of 'audible sounds'
Class of 1915 youths
And that electrified wire
Don't weep then for the horrors of war
Before it we had only
The surface of the earth and seas
After it we'll have the depths
The subsoil and the flight of space
Masters at the helm
Afterwards afterwards
We'll taste the joys
Of victors at their ease
Women Games Factories Commerce
Industry Agriculture Metal
Fire Crystal Speed
Voice Look Touch apart
Together in the far-off sense of touch
And farther still
Far beyond this earth

LA JOLIE ROUSSE

Me voici devant tous un homme plein de sens
Connaissant la vie et de la mort ce qu'un vivant peut
connaître
Ayant éprouvé les douleurs et les joies de l'amour
Ayant su quelquefois imposer ses idées
Connaissant plusieurs langages
Ayant pas mal voyagé
Ayant vu la guerre dans l'Artillerie et l'Infanterie
Blessé à la tête Trépané sous le chloroforme
Ayant perdu ses meilleurs amis dans l'effroyable lutte
Je sais d'ancien et de nouveau autant qu'un homme seul
porrait des deux savoir
Et sans m'inquiéter aujourd'hui de cette guerre
Entre nous et pour nous mes amis
Je juge cette longue querelle de la tradition et de
l'invention
De l'Ordre et de l'Aventure

Vous dont la bouche est faite à l'image de celle de Dieu
Bouche qui est l'ordre même
Soyez indulgents quand vous nous comparez
A ceux qui furent la perfection de l'ordre
Nous qui quêtons partout l'aventure

THE PRETTY REDHEAD

Here I am a man of sense in front of everyone
Knowing life and all of death that a living man can know
Having felt the miseries and joys of love
Having known sometimes how to force his own ideas
Knowing several languages
Quite well-travelled
Having seen the war in artillery and infantry
Wounded in the head trepanned under chloroform
Having lost his best friends in the terrible slaughter
I know of the old and of the new as much as any man
alone might know of both
And without unsettling myself today about this war
Between us and for us my friends
I adjudicate this age-old quarrel between tradition and
invention
Order and Adventure

You whose mouth is made in God's image
Mouth which is order itself
Be forgiving when you judge us
With those who were the perfection of order
We who look everywhere for adventure

Nous ne sommes pas vos ennemis
Nous voulons vous donner de vastes et d'étranges
domaines
Où le mystère en fleurs s'offre à qui veut le cueillir
Il y a là des feux nouveaux des couleurs jamais vues
Mille phantasmes impondérables
Auxquels il faut donner de la réalité

Nous voulons explorer la bonté contrée énorme
où tout se tait
Il ya a aussi le temps qu'on peut chasser ou faire revenir
Pitié pour nous qui combattons toujours aux frontières
De l'illimité et de l'avenir
Pitié pour nos erreurs pitié pour nos péchés

Voici que vient l'été la saison violente
Et ma jeunesse est morte ainsi que le printemps
O Soleil c'est le temps de la Raison ardente
Et j'attends
Pour la suivre toujours la forme noble et douce
Qu'elle prend afin que je l'aime seulement
Elle vient et m'attire ainsi qu'un fer l'aimant
Elle a l'aspect charmant
D'une adorable rousse

Ses cheveux sont d'or on dirait
Un bel éclair qui durerait
Ou ces flammes qui se pavanent
Dans les roses-thé qui se fanent

We are not your enemies
We'd like to give you strange and vast domains
Where mystery yields up itself in flowers for those
who wish to gather
New fires are there and colours never seen before
A thousand airy phantoms
Each to be given weight

We wish to explore the huge expanse of excellence
where everything is still
Time as well which one can chase or else retrieve
Have pity for us who fight on the frontiers always
Of the limitless and what's to come
Have pity for our errors and pity for our sins

Here comes the summer the violent season
And my youth is dead as is the spring
This O Sun is the hour of passionate Reason
And I wait always
To follow the soft and exalted form she takes
So as to make me love her only
She comes and attracts me like a magnet
She has the charming look
Of a lovable redhead

Her hair one could say is made of gold
A lovely lightning flash which lasts
Or those flames which strut like peacocks
In the fading tea-roses

Mais riez riez de moi
Hommes de partout surtout gens d'ici
Car il y a tant de choses que je n'ose vous dire
Tant de choses que vous ne me laisseriez pas dire
Ayez pitié de moi

Laugh at me go on and laugh
You men from all over especially here
There are so many things I dare not tell you
So many things you would not let me say
Have pity on me

LA PETITE AUTO

Le 31 du mois d'Août 1914
Je partis de Deauville un peu avant minuit
Dans la petite auto de Rouveyre

Avec son chauffeur nous étions trois

Nous dîmes adieu à toute une époque
Des géants furieux se dressaient sur l'Europe
Les aigles quittaient leur aire attendant le soleil
Les poissons voraces montaient des abîmes
Les peuples accouraient pour se connaître à fond
Les morts tremblaient de peur dans leurs sombres
demeures

Les chiens aboyaient vers là-bas où étaient les frontières
Je m'en allais portant en moi toutes ces armées
qui se battaient
Je les sentais monter en moi et s'étaler les contrées
où elles serpentaient
Avec les forêts les villages heureux de la Belgique
Francorchamps avec l'Eau Rouge et les pouhons
Région par où se font toujours les invasions
Artères ferroviaires où ceux qui s'en allaient mourir
saluaient encore une fois la vie colorée
Océans profonds où remuaient les monstres
Dans les vieilles carcasses naufragées
Hauteurs inimaginables où l'homme combat
Plus haut que l'aigle ne plane
L'homme y combat contre l'homme
Et descend tout à coup comme une étoile filante
Je sentais en moi des êtres neufs pleins de dextérité

THE LITTLE CAR

On the 31st of August 1914
I left Deauville just before midnight
In Rouveyre's little car

With his driver there were three of us

We were saying goodbye to a whole epoch
Raging giants were stirring over Europe
Eagles left their eyries looking for the sun
Ravenous fish were rising from abysses
Whole nations were rushing to know themselves completely
The dead were shivering with fear in their dark lodgings

Dogs were barking towards distant frontiers
I carried within me all the struggling armies
I felt them rise in me and sprawl through regions where
they wound
Among the forests the happy villages of Belgium
Francorchamps l'Eau Rouge Les Pouhons
The place where the invasions are always made
The railway arteries where those about to die
Saluted once more a life full of colour
The ocean depths where monsters moved
Among the skeletons of shipwrecks
Unthought of heights where man is fighting
Higher than the eagle soars
One man in combat with another
Who comes down like a shooting star
I felt within me new beings full of skill

Bâtir et aussi agencer un univers nouveau
Un marchand d'une opulence inouïe et d'une taille
prodigieuse
Disposait un étalage extraordinaire
Et des bergers gigantesques menaient
De grands troupeaux muets qui broutaient les paroles
Et contre lesquels aboyaient tous les chiens sur la route

Je n'oublierai jamais ce voyage nocturne où nul de nous ne dit un mot

O
dé
part
sombre
où mouraient
nos 3 phares

o
nuit
tendre
d'avant
la guerre

o
vil
lages
où
s e h â
t a i e n t

MARECHAUX-FERRANTS RAPPELES

ENTRE MINUIT ET UNE HEURE DU MATIN

v
e r s
L i s i e u x
là très
bleu

ou bien

V
e r s
a i l l e
s d'o
r

et 3 fois nous nous arrêtâmes pour changer un pneu qui avait éclaté

Building a whole new universe and running it too
A merchant of prodigious wealth and size
Was setting out a weird display
Gigantic shepherds drove
Huge flocks which browsed on words
Barked at by all the roadside dogs

I'll never forget this journey by night where none of us said a word

O
dark
departure
when our 3
headlights failed

o
tender
night
before
the war

o
vil
lages towards which h u r r i e d

BLACKSMITHS RECALLED

BETWEEN MIDNIGHT AND ONE IN THE MORNING

n
e a r
L i s i e u x
so very
blue

or else

V
ersa
illes the
gold
en

and 3 times we had to stop to change a blown-out tyre

Et quand après avoir passé l'après-midi
Par Fontainebleau
Nous arrivâmes à Paris
Au moment où l'on affichait la mobilisation
Nous comprîmes mon camarade et moi
Que la petite auto nous avait conduits dans une époque
Nouvelle
Et bien qu'étant déjà tous deux des hommes mûrs
Nous venions cependant de naître

And when having passed that afternoon
Through Fontainebleau
We got to Paris
At the moment the mobilisation was posted
We understood my friend and I
That the little car had brought us into
A completely new age
And although we were both grown men
We had only just been born